AUSTRALIAN INTELLECTUALS:
THEIR STRANGE HISTORY
& PATHOLOGICAL TENDENCIES

By the same author:

Cultural Liberalism in Australia (CUP, 1995)
The Packaging of Australia (UNSW, 1998)
A Short History of Australian Liberalism (CIS, 2001)
The Power of Ideas (ASP, 2009)

AUSTRALIAN INTELLECTUALS

Their strange history
&
pathological tendencies

Greg Melleuish

Connor Court Publishing
Ballan, Australia

CONTENTS

Preface

This small book began life as two papers that I delivered for a conference on Australian intellectuals in 2007 held by the Institute of Public Affairs in Melbourne. It was a very enjoyable day. Since that time I have re-worked both papers so that they have become one. I wish to thank the IPA, and especially John Roskam and Chris Berg, for their hospitality in having me work in the IPA Office both in 2007 and 2011. It is a great place to spend time. I also wish to thank them for the assistance that they have given me reading the manuscript and commenting on it. I also wish to thank the publisher of Connor Court, Anthony Cappello, for the faith which he has shown in my work.

The IPA established its Foundations of Western Civilisation Program in response to the sorts of issues that I raise in the following pages. They recognised that one of the major problems with the life of the mind in contemporary Australia is the way in which it disparages and disrespects the extraordinary rich intellectual and cultural tradition which we, in Australia, have been fortunate enough to inherit from Western Civilisation. Why should those who have been entrusted with the preservation of those intellectual riches, such as humanities academics in our publicly funded universities, not only fail to do their job but also treat their inheritance in such a fashion? Surely if, to paraphrase Burke, there is a compact between our ancestors, ourselves and our descendants, those of us entrusted with the responsibility of teaching about and writing on the things of the mind should treat our inheritance with respect and ensure that it is passed on to the next generation in good repair.

That certainly was how our ancestors who came to Australia in the nineteenth century saw their role. That is why they established universities and not technical colleges or training institutes. As I argue, something began to go wrong in the early twentieth century, and that something has only got worse over the past one hundred years. Whereas once we had a smallish group of people devoted to ideas in Australia, many of whom did not have university degrees, now we have an enormous 'intellectual class' largely composed of professional academics. The extraordinary thing is that as the number of university educated increases, the quality of our public intellectual life declines. None of our newspapers today can match in quality the leading articles of men such as John West and Andrew Garran in the *Sydney Morning Herald* of the 1860s and 1870s. We are now addicted to spin, excessive rhetoric and the KISS principle. All of this has happened despite more and more graduates being churned out of our universities.

Producing more and more graduates does not create what Donald Horne termed the 'clever country', exactly the opposite. One must surely wonder why this should be the case. And the responsibility must come back to the intellectual class. They tend to have very negative attitudes to both the society in which they live and the wonderful traditions to which it is heir. It may be that they feel that their worth is not properly appreciated; certainly they have a strong streak of narcissism about them. They have an attitude problem.

A strong and confident society needs to feel comfortable about where it came from and to where it is going. This does not mean that it cannot be critical of its traditions, after all that is what the Western intellectual tradition has always been since the time of Socrates, but it cannot afford to sink into a mire of negativity. That is the road to nihilism. Only a proper and balanced appreciation of our intellectual and cultural heritage will prevent us from going down that road. There are glimmers of hope, such as the recent re-awakening of interest in Western civilisation as exemplified by the IPA program and the establishment of Campion College as a liberal arts institution dedicated to teaching about the traditions of Western civilisation.

The great hope is to be found amongst young people. I find that they come to university wanting to study about the traditions of the West, including Ancient Greece and Rome. Other cultures, including China, know and appreciate how important Western traditions are. It seems only to be our intellectual class, so wrapped up in its own pre-occupations, who cannot see the riches sitting in front of them.

1

Introduction

In the wake of the defeat of the Commonwealth Coalition Government headed by John Howard in 2007 arguments emerged that the culture wars that were so significant for Australian public life in recent times were over. For such people, Kevin Rudd represented a new chapter in Australian history, a new synthesis that reconciled the two sides of the dialectic, or so it would appear to some who live in the foggy world of the Left. Of course, it is nonsense to believe that an empirical event like an election can somehow dramatically change the *geist* of a nation, but it is not unreasonable to argue that the policies and actions of a new government would generate new debates and discussions.

A new chapter of the culture wars in Australia began with the accession of Rudd to power and has continued with his successor Julia Gillard. The war has remained the same even as some of the sites of conflict have changed. Now the issues relate to climate change, the Carbon Tax, Media Freedom and the overall competence of the Commonwealth government to deliver anything in a competent fashion, be it an education revolution, insulation in the ceiling or a national broadband network. Some issues, such as those relating to education, remain the same. In the 'culture wars', as in so much of human affairs, there is no 'end of history', just a continuing debate and conflict of ideas.

What we today call culture wars would appear to be a normal part of the human condition as human beings have always had a propensity to disagree about intellectual matters, dating back to the dialogues of Plato and their record of Socrates' discussions with the sophists. The ancient world saw the development of a range of philosophical schools while the early Christian Church was torn apart by a range of theological disputes that can only properly be described as 'culture wars'.

In many ways the conflict between Augustine and Pelagius over the capacity of human beings to achieve grace through their own efforts can be seen as emblematic of the form that culture wars have taken ever since that time in the West. On the one hand there are liberals who have a faith in the capacity of human action to achieve a good outcome through their own unaided efforts. On the other hand there are conservatives who are impressed by the limitations of human nature and argue that attempts to change radically the human condition are as likely to produce evil as good.

As W.S. Gilbert put it in the nineteenth century, all human beings are born either little liberals or little conservatives. Of course, in contemporary terms, this translates into Left and Right. The culture wars, the never ending disputes of intellectuals, are no more than the consequence of this fact. Where there are intellectuals there will be conflict. This reflects no more than the diversity of human nature, that individuals possess different attitudes and dispositions. As long as there are human beings there will be disagreements and a desire by individuals to prove that they are right. The major issue is to ensure that these conflicts provide benefits rather than pain for the rest of the citizens of our country.

Intellectuals, especially those of a Left disposition, can be seen as being obsessed with the primacy of the cognitive, even to the point of being pathological. Whereas carpenters are skilled workers of wood and cooks express their ability through their command of the culinary arts, so intellectuals place the highest importance on ideas. They tend to believe that human beings should, and can, be made to conform to a set of clear ideas. The effects of reforming human beings through the implementation of clear and apparently simple ideas, through the attempt to create a 'new man', can be seen in the destructive effects of communism and fascism in the twentieth century.

Yet it must also be recognised that in any healthy society intellectual debates are necessary and that they should be welcomed as the best way of dealing with matters of public concern. Such debates can turn acrimonious from time to time, and thereby appear to take on the appearance of 'wars'. This may be regrettable but probably they cannot be avoided given the frailties of human nature. The ideal would be to adopt a balanced approach to the study of human affairs, an approach that diluted the power of intellectual abstraction with an appreciation of the complex and ambiguous nature of reality. It would be a liberalism tempered by conservatism. But human beings invariably go to extremes; much as they may preach the virtues of moderation and the 'golden mean' they cannot help fighting over who is right and who is wrong.

The first section of this essay deals with the broad question of the role of intellectuals generally in Australian since the nineteenth century to today while the second part considers the particular case of history. In many ways history constitutes a special case in

Australian intellectual life because it has assumed great prominence for governments when they have considered the appropriate curriculum for Australian school students in the twenty-first century. In Australia it is not philosophy or the social sciences which has taken that niche in the curriculum that is reserved for the study of culture. It is history. Historians have a role in Australian public culture that far exceeds that of philosophers or political scientists. They have set themselves up as the prophets of the civil religion of the nation and are treated accordingly.

If anything, the increased government interest in history has raised the stakes regarding the outcome of the culture wars. It can be argued that whoever wins the battle about the nature of the past is always in a strong position to win that of the future. However, the last thing that any sensible person wants is a future dominated by intellectual abstractions that have little foundation in empirical reality and are driven by the obsessive concerns of intellectuals seeking to shape the world according to their intellectual fantasies. That way lays the madness of Lenin, Stalin and Pol Pot. One way to guard against such a possibility is to have a sound appreciation of the role of intellectuals in the development of Australian culture, and, in particular, to appreciate the centrality of history to intellectual life in Australia.

2

Intellectuals in Australia: An Historical Sketch

The way in which one understands the role of intellectuals in society is determined, at least in part, by how one views intellectuals as either a force for good or otherwise. This means having an understanding of what exactly one means by the term 'intellectual'. It is often argued that Anglo-sphere societies either do not have intellectuals or are anti-intellectual in that they mistrust ideas and their capacity to effect change.[1] In part this goes back to the Enlightenment and the French Revolution. If the archetypical modern intellectual is the *philosophe*, the product of the French Enlightenment, then it can be doubted if the English have really ever had intellectuals at all. The English complaint from Edmund Burke to Matthew Arnold was that abstract ideas took a Jacobin form, thereby leading to attempts at radical change and its ensuing social disorder.

The *philosophes* all too often stood at odds with the world of which they were part, seeking in some shape or form to subvert it. They were part of the radical Enlightenment that looked back to Pierre Bayle and the republicans and Deists of the seventeenth century. Hidden from sight in eighteenth century Paris, were the

---

1 Stefan Collini, *Absent Minds: Intellectuals in Britain,* Oxford University Press, Oxford, 2006.

pornographers and hacks of Grub Street, plying their tacky trade, who believed that intellectual liberty meant freedom to libel. Part of the problem in France, as in other continental countries, was that a gulf existed between intellectuals and those holding positions of authority, a gulf that was exacerbated by the fact that many of the ideas advocated by the *philosophes* were seen to be subversive of the existing order.

François Furet, following Cochin, has argued that part of the problem with the leading lights of the French Revolution was that, in the days before the Revolution, they were used to debating topics in provincial academies rather than solving practical problems.[2] They came to see politics in terms of rhetoric rather than practice. When the Revolution came they struggled to control the flow of events through controlling political rhetoric. Words rather than deeds became central to their political activity and they came to see anyone who disagreed with them as an enemy only worthy of extermination. In a sense the French Revolution pioneered an early version of political correctness, only with deadly consequences for those who lost the battle of rhetoric.

This was not so much the case in Britain where men of ideas could enjoy preferment and come to occupy positions of prestige and power. When one considers the Scottish Enlightenment one is struck most by its moderation, and by the fact that many of its key figures held posts at Scottish universities. The Anglo-sphere world has been considered to have fostered the moderate Enlightenment, the Enlightenment of Locke and of the pursuit of tolerance and

---

2 François Furet, *Interpreting the French Revolution*, Trans. Elborg Forster, Cambridge University press, Cambridge, 198.

civility, characterised by sweet commerce, that followed in the wake of the Glorious Revolution of 1688.[3] There continued to be in England a connection in the eighteenth and nineteenth centuries between the educated man and the realm of public affairs, in terms of the church, the universities and the political world. England did not foster the sort of environment in which intellectuals devoted to opposing the establishment could flourish. There was a place for them in the public sphere. This is perhaps why it has been believed that England has never had real intellectuals.

Even in Australia, it must be said, the need for men of intellect and scholarship was not ignored during the nineteenth century, in the same way as colonial Australia came to embody many of the principles of the moderate Enlightenment.[4] This can be seen in the fact that as the prospect of a measure of self-government became likely in the late 1840s colonial leaders such as W.C. Wentworth worked to establish a local university. Wentworth's purpose was to produce those sorts of educated men who could provide leadership for colonial society. This was a goal that was later endorsed by Sir Henry Parkes, who believed that the leadership of a democracy should come, as far as possible, from the group of educated gentlemen. By the 1870s the University of Sydney and the University of Melbourne had established University Unions with the purpose of providing young men with the opportunity to hone the sorts of skills that they would need in public life. Under the leadership of its early Principals such as John Woolley and Charles

---

3 For the distinction between radical and moderate Enlightenment see Jonathan I Israel, *Enlightenment Contested: Philosophy, Modernity, and the Emancipation of Man 1670–1752*, Oxford University Press, Oxford, 2006.
4 John Gascoigne with the assistance of Patricia Curthoys, *The Enlightenment and the origins of European Australia*, Cambridge University Press, Cambridge, 2002.

Badham the University of Sydney saw itself as producing future political leaders, which it did in the shape of Samuel Griffith and Edmund Barton. Equally the University of Melbourne produced a future Prime Minister in the shape of Alfred Deakin.

There were intellectual circles in nineteenth century Australia, such as the Stenhouse literary circle in Sydney, various mechanics institutes dedicated to 'self culture' and the groups of colonial gentlemen who sought to foster a practical interest in the sciences. Many colonials pursued the life of the mind alongside their practical callings, be it in the arts or the sciences. Finally there were the many newspapers and magazines established in colonial Australia that were often of higher quality intellectually than those produced today.

There is a mythology that men of letters in the nineteenth century Australian colonies bravely struggled in a philistine and materialist society, often being destroyed in the process. One thinks of Daniel Deniehy or Henry Kendall or Charles Harpur. The market for poets and litterateurs in Australia was limited, but that does not mean that the life of the mind was neglected. It was just that it was not possible for one to pursue literary and intellectual activities full time in a small developing society in which everyone had to work for a living. Rather what we had in nineteenth century Australia was a rather remarkable collection of highly intelligent politicians, newspaper editors, clerics, teachers and lawyers who wrote with intelligence and verve on a whole range of topics, many of them associated with the practical affairs of the day. The level of discussion conducted by both John West and his successor Andrew Garran as editors at the *Sydney Morning*

Herald was extraordinarily high. Many of their editorials read like mini essays in politics, economics and even political theory. Both Alfred Deakin and Charles Pearson, who wrote for *The Age* in Melbourne, maintained similar high standards of discussion.

Many politicians, who were often also barristers, contributed thoughtful, intelligent articles of high standard to the press and local journals or made speeches that are marked by a very high degree of sophistication. On reading some of the speeches and newspaper articles of Henry Parkes, by no means a highly educated man, one cannot but be struck by both the force of his mind and his analytical capacities. In fact, it can be argued that the body of work produced by nineteenth century liberals in Australia, from West and Garran to William Forster to B.R. Wise to Bruce Smith is unmatched by any of the work on politics and political theory in twentieth century Australia.

Although these men were often critical of the way in which colonial politics and society were moving, they did not become adversarial intellectuals seeking to 'oppose the system'. They were practical men working in their way to improve the world around them. Nor were they opposed to culture and the arts. It has been claimed that in New South Wales 'there was something of a poetry mafia in nineteenth century government circles'.[5] A figure such as Bede Dalley who pursued both political and literary interests sought to provide patronage for the poet Henry Kendall. When Kendall died Dalley gave a lecture on Edmund Burke and Charles Badham a lecture on Dante to raise money for Kendall's family.

---

5 Hilary Golder, Politics, Patronage and Public Works: *The Administration of New South Wales, volume 1, 1842–1900*, University of New South Wales Press, 2005, p. 210.

Henry Parkes published several volumes of (bad) verse while even George Reid, often stigmatised as a philistine, published an ode on the Sydney International Exhibition and was one of the subscribers who made the publication of Christopher Brennan's *Poems 1913* possible.

The real birth of the adversarial intellectual in Australia may be dated to the establishment of *The Bulletin*, and in particular the direction that it took under J.F. Archibald. *The Bulletin* was 'agin' the respectable bourgeois world of late nineteenth century Australia. It took up the cudgels against politicians, capitalists, monarchists, supporters of empire, religion and women. *The Bulletin* was, in many ways, a pale reflection of the radical Enlightenment and of the vituperative polemics of Grub Street, with the new irrationalism of the nineteenth century *fin de siècle* tacked on. The flourishing of *The Bulletin* coincided with the birth of the Labor Party in Australia and the first real advocacy of socialist ideas. The mélange of ideas that floated around in the 1890s and were often taken up by the 'Bully' represent the first real expression of adversarial culture in Australia and the first opening up of the gap between the mainstream and the rest, with the emergence of a Bohemian, *avant garde* sub-culture in Sydney and Melbourne.

This is not to say that men of ideas ceased to be involved in public life or to contribute to the life of the nation. One could point to the contribution of the Round Table, a group of eminent intellectuals who formed part of a British imperial network, and who analysed public affairs for the *Round Table* magazine during the first half of the twentieth century. There were, however, some problems. One was the limited opportunities for men and women of ideas in Australia. The number of universities was small and the number of positions in them limited. The same was true of the press. For many years the Commonwealth public service was opposed to the recruitment of university graduates, preferring after World War I to take ex-servicemen. When it finally decided to employ graduates it put a limit on the number that could be employed. The market for literature was limited both by the size of the population and the competition provided by other English speaking countries. A small number of Australian intellectuals did manage to exercise considerable influence on public matters in the inter-war years, thereby keeping alive the nineteenth century ideals of public service by educated men. These included economists such as L.F. Giblin and J.B. Brigden and the anthropologist and cleric A.P. Elkin in the field of Aboriginal policy. One can also point to the influence of the essays written by Walter Murdoch.

Many Australians with intellectual interests left the country from the late nineteenth century through to the mid-twentieth century. This is what one would expect to happen in a province of an empire; the metropolis beckoned, not to mention America. Such figures included Samuel Alexander, Gilbert Murray, Grafton Elliot Smith, Jack Lindsay, Vere Gordon Childe, W.K. Hancock, Persia Campbell. One could say, as a sort of general rule, that many of those thinkers who left Australia were not only talented but also broad minded. Those who were left behind, or who returned to Australia, such as P.R. Stephensen, were often rabid nationalists who pleaded their own cause using nationalist sentiments. Hence Stephensen's *Foundations of Culture in Australia*, essentially a nationalist rant, was written in the wake of his failure as a publisher. Of course, this was not universally true. Academics such V.G. Portus or A.R. Chisholm and a figure such as Bishop Burgmann could take a much more European or even world perspective from within Australia. Still, for many would be men and women of ideas in Australia there was a great temptation to adopt an adversarial position and to associate that adversarial role with an advocacy of Australian nationalism.

Moreover there were many who fell under the spell of the Revolution of 1917 and a few who were attracted to its right wing equivalent in the shape of fascism. It can be said that in Australia, as elsewhere in the Western world, the years after World War I saw disillusionment with liberalism, democracy and capitalism. It is sometimes easy to forget how close liberal democracy came to being extinguished in Europe during the 1930s and 1940s.

Marxism seduced many Australian intellectuals in the years between the two World Wars. In a way this was connected to what is called, correctly or otherwise, the secularisation of the Australian 'thinking classes'. Many Australian thinkers in the nineteenth century came either from a clerical background or had religious beliefs. Towards the end of the nineteenth century many of the educated tended to move away from traditional Christianity into other forms of religious expression. These included spiritualism, liberal Christianity, Theosophy and various other forms of nature mysticism including forms of environmentalism. This move towards 'spirituality' is something that continues today and has been remarked upon by Ronald Inglehart and Christian Welzel as a feature of contemporary democracy.[6]

---

6 Ronald Inglehart and Christian Welzel, *Modernization, Cultural Change, and Democracy: The Human Development Sequence*, Cambridge University Press, Cambridge, 2005, pp. 31–2.

In the early twentieth century this development was connected with an interest in eugenics and a movement away, in certain quarters, from religion to political religion, the Australia equivalent of what Michael Burleigh has described as occurring in Europe at the same time.[7] The appeal of Marxism was twofold in that it offered both a critique of what many young people who experienced either World War I or the Depression saw as a corrupt and evil world and a hope of a future in which the sins of the present would be washed away. It justified an anti-bourgeois attitude and an excuse to hate the respectability of their parents.

Adversarial culture in the Australia of the 1920s and 1930s had both an *avant garde* dimension and a Marxist dimension. They were united by a hatred of the bourgeoisie. This can be seen in the figure of John Anderson in the years immediately following his arrival in Sydney in 1927. Anderson was both a Marxist and a scourge of the respectable members of Australian society, encouraging students to mock the traditions of their society and advocating new modernist ideas. However, while Anderson was slowly making his way from communism to Trotskyism to liberalism and classicism he left behind him a group known as the Libertarians that turned its back on the wider world so that it could engage in endless pub discussions and free love.

The Marxists did not have the field to themselves. On the right there was an adversarial culture that owed something to both the Catholic Church and the ideas of French thinker and leader of the *Action Française* Charles Maurras. There were a small

---

7 Michael Burleigh, *Sacred Causes: Religion and Politics from the European Dictators to Al Quaeda*, HarperCollins, London, 2006

group of Australian Maurassians, but what they absorbed from Maurras was neither his integral nationalism nor his anti-Semitism. Rather what they took from him was an idealisation of Latin civilisation, an idealisation not all that different to that found in T.S. Eliot or E.R. Curtius. This idealisation of the Latin West was very easily combined with support for the Catholic Church as the bastion of Western civilisation against the Communist threat. But these intellectuals were hardly supporters of either liberalism or capitalism. A.R. Chisholm was a Maurassian with sympathy for the classicism of the Catholic Church but he could not bring himself to convert to Catholicism. His friend, Carl Kaeppel, however, did take the plunge and convert. There were a small number of other converts to Catholicism amongst Australian intellectuals, including Adela Pankhurst Walsh and, most famously of all, James McAuley. Now McAuley was not a Maurrasian but he imbibed the ideals of classicism as a student of Anderson and through reading Jacques Maritain. There were also Maurassian elements in the Campion circles of the 1930s in Melbourne. It should also be pointed out that Anderson was a Classicist in the Maurassian sense, and that it was this classicism that made it so easy for Andersonians and Catholics to come together in *Quadrant*.

What appears to have been happening in Australia during these years was a sundering of a large number of Australian intellectuals into two groups on the right and the left, neither of whom were greatly impressed with the achievements of liberalism or capitalism. Where, one may well ask, were the liberals of the centre, speaking up in defence of liberal Australia? The one great book in favour of liberal Australia was Hancock's *Australia* published in 1930. It was essentially a critique of the way in which Australia had moved in the early twentieth century to a more statist and protectionist political culture. It was Hancock's 'liberal' book; he subsequently moved more to the left as he departed Australia to take up a position in England.

Hancock used the work of two other important Australian liberals, Frederic Eggleston and Edward Shann. Eggleston was critical of the way in which state socialist enterprises had developed in Victoria while Shann was the great advocate of free trade as the means to national strength. Shann, however, was soon dead, while Eggleston was essentially a survivor of nineteenth century liberalism, having been born in 1870. Intellectually liberalism, capitalism and democracy were on the back foot in the years leading up to the Second World War. Leaving aside Eggleston's *Search for a Social Philosophy*, it is difficult to discover a robust defence of liberalism and liberal democracy during these years.

World War II had an effect on some of this. The war, and the existence of a federal Labor Government, encouraged many Left intellectuals to place a faith in the capacity of state planning to solve social problems and even to join the Commonwealth government to work for that goal. This had the effect of stimulating some thinkers to consider the role of the state just as Hayek did in the same period when he wrote *The Road to Serfdom*. The closest to this work in Australia was John Anderson's essay on the Servile State in which he emphasised the way in which the planned welfare state discouraged the active intellectual life.[8] This was part of Anderson's

---

8 John Anderson, 'The Servile State', in his *Studies in Empirical Philosophy*, Angus and Robertson, Sydney, 1962, pp. 328-339.

movement towards a more liberal position but it also pushed him and his supporters into a ghetto where they struggled to preserve the life of the mind against what they saw as a hostile outside world.

This was also the environment in which, in a different setting, the Institute of Public Affairs was born. In its pioneering work, *Looking Forward: A Post War Policy for Australian Industry*, the Institute argued against the constrictive nature of the regulative state that attempted to implement a planned economy, arguing that such a move was undemocratic and laid the foundation for totalitarianism. Like Anderson this work emphasised the importance of effort and risk, except that it associated these values with free enterprise and its capacity to foster freedom of initiative and a spirit of adventure.[9]

It would be true to say, however, that the growing encroachment of the state on the lives of Australians was generally welcomed by Australian intellectuals. The Left was challenged intellectually less by liberals than by Catholics. It is interesting in reading Manning Clark that while he had nothing but contempt for the solid, if somewhat unromantic, values of British Protestants, he respected Catholicism.

The need to combat Communism also clearly had an impact. There was a need for a common front against Communism and to enunciate those values for which the West, and Australia as part of the West, stood. The consequence was that if the late nineteenth century was the golden age of liberal intellectual life in Australia, the second half of the twentieth century was the golden

---

9 *Looking Forward: A Post War Policy for Australian Industry,* Institute of Public Affairs, 1944, pp. 31, 13, 21.

age of conservatism, at least as measured by the production of significant books. The key figure was, of course, B.A. Santamaria, who opposed Communism and advocated Catholic social doctrine both politically and intellectually. But there were major works of conservative thought produced. Amongst these works James McAuley's *The End of Modernity* stands out. McAuley provided an unrelenting criticism of the defects of modern civilisation combined with a defence of the religious view of the world that scandalised secular intellectuals. But, Santamaria and McAuley suffered from vilification by the Left. *The End of Modernity*, which is truly an Australian intellectual classic, has never enjoyed the reputation that it deserves. As well, in the 1970s and beyond, there were the various books of Ronald Conway that took a softer more Gnostic approach and the astringent critique of humanism by John Carroll.

When the new journal *Quadrant* was established in 1956 with McAuley as its editor, to provide an intellectual alternative to communist and other leftist writing, the key to its intellectual vitality can be seen in its bringing together Catholics and Andersonians. The key to this apparently strange alliance was both their opposition to the deformities of communism and their adherence to classical values. Anderson was a consistent advocate of classical values and a critic of Romanticism. The implication of this adherence to classicism has been a belief in a natural order that provides the measure for human life. Hence McAuley could write:

> The normal condition of the arts corresponds to a normal condition of society; one implies the other. By normal, I mean in the first place that most societies at most times

exhibit certain constant characteristics, and that the same is true of their arts. But it is also implied that these constant characteristics furnish a norm, a rule of health and well-being: in short, a natural order, in the sense that it is an order appropriate to man's natural constitution.[10]

This faith in a classical world that is ordered according to certain principles that are appropriate to human nature has sustained *Quadrant* and much of the non-Left intelligentsia in Australia since the 1950s. It has led to a consistent rejection of the innovations of the Left that seek to transform the world according to ideas that are determined not by an appeal to tradition and the natural order but to some sort of utopian fantasy. In this sense this is no more than a continuation of the war first begun by the nominalists in the thirteenth century. The post-modernists, like the Marxists before them, and the Romantics before them, believe that human beings can be transformed through an act of human will. But if there is a natural order then such acts of will are not only wrong but dangerous.

Those advocating a classical position have remained a minority in Australia. During the second half of the twentieth century, Australian intellectuals not only retained their left orientation, but over time this orientation was reinforced. Conservatives and liberals increasingly looked as if they were becoming an endangered species. The faith that the world can be transformed through an act of will based on a set of abstract ideas has become stronger rather than weaker. Why has this been the case?

The first reason relates to secularisation. Many of the older

---

10 James McAuley, *The End of Modernity,* Angus & Robertson, Sydney, 1959, p. 3

generation of liberal thinkers had either been clerics, had a religious background or were favourable to religion. The newer generations of intellectuals tended either to be agnostic or actively hostile to religion. Secular intellectuals have always had a much greater affinity with the Left. Having rejected Christianity they are attracted to 'political religions' that can provide a substitute eschatology. The appeal of the Left, with its emphasis on the capacity of the will to transform human nature, is that it provides such a substitute. It takes from God and gives to man. It makes intellectuals into important people. It is worthwhile noting that Eggleston's defence of liberalism, published at the beginning of World War II, and in many ways the last great such attempt in Australia, invoked the Christian ethic.

The second reason relates to the tendency for intellectuals to be increasingly associated with universities and to be isolated in academic ghettos from the world of mainstream Australia. Academics have tended to congregate in the inner suburbs of the large cities with people of like mind. As the number of universities, and the number of people they employed, expanded in the 1960s an academic/intellectual subculture emerged in Australia that was in many ways self-sufficient and could ignore the wider world. Academic self-interest has meant that leftist intellectuals are in favour of government intervention as both their teaching and research careers are largely dependent on funds that they receive from government sources.

Given these institutional and cultural factors, one can point to the development of an intellectual subculture from the 1960s onwards. This subculture came to reproduce itself through its academic structures and is largely based on humanities and social science academics. Over time it became stronger and more narrow and homogeneous in its political and cultural outlook as those who did not share its views either opted out or were excluded. It partly overlaps with subcultures in the media and the *avant garde* art world with which it shares a number of common values. However, it tends to be at some distance from the world of public affairs and a long way from mainstream Australia.

While there had been small intellectual/artistic groups in the past that had developed an adversarial culture they were too small and lacked institutional stability to exercise much influence over the wider culture. The permanent establishment of a large number of publicly funded universities provided the pre-condition for an equally permanent adversarial culture.

It is important to realise that the growth and dominance of a left adversarial subculture can be explained as a natural social development, largely in terms of individual self-interest. The intellectual Left has come, over time, to form a veritable intellectual cartel as it has slowly but surely captured more and more of the institutions of the mind in Australia, including the ABC. It is difficult for a genuine liberal who is willing to reward ability and hard work regardless of ideology to survive in such an environment. He, or she, will soon discover that others do not play by those rules; holding a particular view is regarded as an indication of person's ability. Any individual who seriously contemplates a career in these sorts of areas has to consider their options very seriously. In universities they have to run the gauntlet of completing a higher degree and then competing for jobs. The options are limited. The easiest way to go is to run with the pack. Universities believe in every sort of 'diversity' except intellectual diversity. As the old joke goes; what is the opposite of diversity? University. Anyone seriously interested in intellectual pluralism in Australia needs to consider how this cartel could most effectively be broken up.

Liberal and conservative thinkers do not have a similar institutional base on which to found a competing culture. They have been outnumbered in the universities and often find the new academic culture not particularly congenial. At times it can be decidedly hostile when the natives decided to be excessively restless. Experience tells such people that they should be very careful about what they say in a university. The notorious Marxist intellectual Herbert Marcuse coined the termed 'repressive tolerance' in the 1960s. The one place where this concept applies is the academic world. Non-conformers are tolerated but it is expected that they will act as self-censors. Working in such an environment can be particularly depressing which is perhaps why any liberal or conservative who wishes to remain moderately sane may decide that a university is not the place to be.

Slowly a weak institutional base for conservative and liberal thinkers emerged in the shape of *Quadrant* magazine, the two major think tanks, the Institute of Public Affairs and the Centre for Independent Studies and other informal groups and dining parties. But these institutions provide little in the way of paid employment and opportunities for advancement as intellectuals. Non-left academics in the universities continue to enjoy an often precarious existence, eyed suspiciously by their colleagues and never really considered to be part of the club. The lack of a strong liberal and conservative culture has meant that non-left intellectuals also lack a market to read their work; conservative and liberal intellectuals do not produce work that is inferior to that written by the left but they lack the sort of guaranteed audience that the left subculture provides, not least through reading lists for university courses.

In some ways the growing intellectual power of the left over the past fifty years, in Australia as in other parts of the world, can be seen as the dominance of the radical enlightenment over the moderate enlightenment. One feature of this dominance has been the rejection of ideas that come from Anglo-sphere societies in favour of those that come from continental Europe, be they French literary theorists or German philosophers. The moderate enlightenment always sought to reconcile the great body of ideas, beliefs and ways of doing things that we have inherited from the past with the new discoveries of the sciences. The radical enlightenment, from the seventeenth century until today, has little or no time for tradition and wants to make the world anew on the basis of abstract, and usually untried, theories. Moreover they believe that it is possible to inflict those theories on the world through an act of will.

We should fear this growing dominance of the abstract over the concrete and of an adversarial culture over one that seeks to reconcile ideas and the practical realities of the world. Intellectuals and intellectual life of this type will do little for the future of Australia. These intellectuals are instinctively Platonists and Gnostics; they perceive themselves to have access to ideas that are superior because unlike the rest of us they have seen the light while we see only shadows. Their ideas need to be imposed on the real world. When one looks at the contemporary humanities faculties of our universities one sees that they are increasingly addicted to theory, and to making the world bend to their theories. It is this combination of abstraction and a faith in the capacity of the will to impose these abstractions on the world that makes these intellectuals such a threat to the contemporary world. It is a world from which they are increasingly divorced physically, living, as they do, in the ghettos that are the creation of their success in the world.

Just how frightening the situation is can be seen in two current issues that have important practical consequences for Australia. These are man-made climate change and the desire for the current government to regulate the flow of ideas as exemplified by the Finkelstein Report. In both case academics have played, and continue to play, a crucial role, and it must be said that their role has not been on the side of the angels.

Climate change has largely been pushed by academics and their allies in the media, especially the ABC. Why has climate change proved to be so popular amongst academia as a group? I think that there are a number of answers:

- The first is naked self-interest. Modern academia is about publishing papers and winning grants as a means of self-advancement. They have discovered that with climate change they are on a real winner. They can claim that the government needs to funds them so that they can find ways of overcoming the effects of climate change, even reverse it. It becomes the 'magic pudding' of research. Enough can never be done. There is always a need for more research, for more grants. The more that is done on climate change the more that needs to be done. As a research topic it appears to be a topic that can be milked forever.

- The second is that as a topic it is an expression of the academic desire to reduce the world to a series of models that can be manipulated to predict the future. Climate change relies heavily on computer modelling, on the assumption that if one feeds in enough information one can create a model that actually depicts reality. The Soviets believed in this fantasy. They sought to build a super computer that would be able to create a model thereby allowing the state to predict the demand in every item used by its people. The model came unstuck on platform shoes. In the seventies platform shoes came into popularity so the Soviets set about planning to produce these shoes. The only problem was that by the time they had them ready the fashion had changed. We live a world that is both complex and contingent. It is a delusion to believe that we can create a model that depicts reality in such a way that we can control the future. When we attempt to do so we simply remain in the abstract world of the model and become its slave.

- The third is a form of moral panic that seems to have overcome many academics. A major discovery of the past one hundred years is that education and devotion to intellectual matters does not make modern human beings more rational. Academics, like other people, are prone to scares and panics, and hence to use their intellects in defence of irrational projects. In Germany the Nazis conquered the students before the rest of the country. Two intellectual giants, Martin Heidegger and Carl Schmitt, came out in support of the Nazis. It could be argued that it is their addiction to abstract models that make academics more prone to emotional manipulation as they do not often possess a well-developed sense of balance between their rational and emotional natures. The more one is addicted to abstract models, the less defence one has against one's irrational urges.

What we can see in academic support for climate change is an emotional zeal combined with a highly developed form of abstract thought that is not very healthy, especially when it is combined with a strong sense of self-interest. What I am arguing is that academic abstraction makes academics more prone to millennial aspirations, and the belief that they can save the world. In his recent book on millennialism Richard Landes argues that millennial movements become more extreme the more that they fail and it will certainly be the case that this is what happens with the climate change lobby.[11] Empirical evidence will have little effect on their views and they will cling to the faith for as long as possible. As this faith is founded on their models, they will come more and more to rely on the models and ignore the real world. And they will become more determined to impose their views on any recalcitrant unbeliever.

The zeal with which academics pursue their defence of climate change is a reminder that many of them are more interested in imposing their views on the wider population than they are in allowing for freedom of speech and expression. Academics, like many other intellectuals, have a very high opinion of themselves and their rightness. Humility is not a virtue in their world. If you are right and you have good intentions then surely you should not only be heard but should also prevail. In fact you probably believe

11 David Landes, *Heaven on Earth: The Varieties of the Millennial Experience*, Oxford University Press, New York, 2011.

that you have a duty to prevail and to drown out the views of those who lack your qualifications and capacity to employ models. They are just inferiors who need to be brought into line.

Such an attitude has long defined how climate change alarmists see their critics and the wider society. Such people should be like their students who are there simply to listen and absorb, not to answer back. Unfortunately this attitude seems now to have spread to government circles in Australia which, under the direction of Julia Gillard and the Greens, are not interested in listening to criticism of their plans but instead think only of ways of preventing their critics from being heard. They have decided; it is the task of the rest of us to obey.

The government and their academic allies use a number of tactics to achieve this goal. One is to de-legitimise anyone who is not considered to be an expert in the field. This was a trick that was used in the History Wars by the Black Armband brigade to attack those who were not 'professional historians'. It has been used to attack climate sceptics by claiming that they do not publish in the peer reviewed journals that are controlled by the climate alarmists. This view that only the experts have a right to speak is anti-democratic. It assumes that the wider population is a bunch of ignorant bogans. Yet our schools supposedly educate students in science and history so that they can become responsible citizens. One must wonder about the value of such education. And who should decide who is an expert and 'permitted' to speak? Would that require a government licensing board? It would be a board run by academics.

Another tactic is to complain about the 'extremism' of those with whom one does not agree and to condemn their supposed verbal violence. The conversation must be kept 'civil' and the fact that those outside the magic circle of expertise cannot seem to control themselves is a justification for not allowing them to be heard. Of course, governments and academics are never intemperate by definition.

The final tactic is to complain about lack of balance. If a publication decides to argue strongly for a position that is not officially approved then that is being unbalanced. The publisher must be forced to publish alternative views, which is to say views that support the government and its academic allies. It doesn't matter that the government and the academics will not give any time of day to views critical of them. After all, they are right.

Free discussion is a major check on excesses of government power. It must be permitted to follow what arguments it wishes even if, from time to time, it does become a little excessive. The best way to correct excess is to allow for other critics to admonish those who have stepped over the line or for critics to poke fun and ridicule such foolishness. There is inherent in human beings a sense of decency and a desire for moderation. Public opinion has its own corrective mechanisms based on that sense of decency.

Unfortunately academics often fail to have respect for the common sense of everyman and everywoman. They are addicted to their abstract models and this prevents them from having a sensible and practical approach to dealing with people. This probably explains why they have failed to come out and condemn the Finkelstein Report. What one sees instead is a measure of support for its recommendations. The obvious reason for this support is that those recommendations will bring certain academics into an alliance with the government. Together they will be able to tame the dark outside forces that stand in the way of their desire to re-make the world in the image of their abstract models.

This is what might be termed the East German syndrome; an alliance between academics and the state for their mutual benefit. Why be critical of the government when it is the government that hands out research funding, jobs and other goodies? Academics know on which side their bread is buttered. After all bureaucrats are also addicted to abstract models of the society they are employed to administer. It is a marriage made in heaven.

What we need now more than ever is a space where the heirs of the moderate Enlightenment and the believers in a natural order can flourish. By that I mean those who know that the relationship between ideas and the real world is a complex one and that when reality refuses to bend to a theory the solution is probably to junk the theory. Ideas and theories are important but we must ensure that they serve our interests rather than us becoming their servants.

The real problem is the way in which the growth of the universities in Australia has been matched by the development of a dominant sub-culture that is both addicted to abstract ideas, or what Matthew Arnold called Jacobinism, and appears to have a stranglehold on the intellectual life of the country. The solution is to break the monopoly of this group so that a genuine pluralism can flourish in Australia. This means recognition that there are other ways of knowing things than the academic view of reality. This means fostering other institutions alongside our public universities so that there is real intellectual diversity in Australia. It means providing the means whereby people outside of officially sanctioned institutions, such as the universities and the ABC, are able to contribute to the public sphere. It means fostering private institutions that can provide genuine intellectual diversity.

If there is any one discipline in Australia that is the 'eye of the storm' of our intellectual problems, then it is surely that of history. It exemplifies so many of the general problems of the humanities and the social sciences. Moreover, over the past decade it has been a battlefield. An academic majority has wielded its 'tyranny of the majority' over a small minority, which has protested about the desire of many of its practitioners to pursue abstract ideas and political agendas at the expense of the facts. It is now to the place of history in Australian intellectual life that we shall now turn.

3

History in Australia

History is not necessarily a discipline that can be described as intellectual in its pretensions. It is not wedded to the tyranny of theory and its abstractions. English historian John Vincent sums this up nicely when he says:

> Apart from a little shoplifting from sociology, historians are uneasy with theory, and have added little to the world of ideas, or to the vocabulary within which ideas can be given form. Intellectually, history is, like classics, a parasite subject.[12]

As the study of history in Australia owes much to its roots in English culture this statement has also largely been true traditionally of historians in this country. History is not a science, or even social science, that traditionally has dealt in abstractions or models. That is not to say that it does not demand intellectual rigour or a capacity to exercise one's analytical capacities. An historian who lazily just reproduces uncritically facts and contemporary accounts from a period is writing something closer to annals than history.

History is a discipline that entails the practice of intellectual skills, but a historian who has only intellectual skills will not be very good at his or her craft. History also requires a capacity for imaginative

---

12 John Vincent, *An Intelligent Person's Guide to History,* Duckworth, London, 1996, p. 69.

empathy, for entering into the position in which the people who one is trying to understand have been placed. Historical study has a powerful hermeneutic element that engages the affective part of our natures. In this sense historians are somewhat like poets and novelists in that they seek to penetrate the surface of human activity and explore both the glories and the darkness that lurk in the human soul.

Unlike poets and novelists historians are bound by the need that what they portray about the past be true, or as close to truth as they can manage. Historians are bound by the evidence that the past has left behind in documents, artifacts and other forms of material survivals. They cannot simply make it up as they go along. In approaching that evidence they must practise critical, even forensic, skills similar to those of a detective or a lawyer seeking to resolve a criminal investigation. Just as Cicero asked *cui bono* so the historian must ask who wrote the document, for what purpose, and in whose interest. Can we believe what it says to be true? The origins of this historical technique lie in that other 'parasitic' subject classics, as humanists subjected classical texts to rigorous scrutiny, declared them to be authentic or not, and demanded emendations where the text seemed to be corrupt.

Having decided which of the evidence passes muster, historians must then exercise skills of a different order as they make use of their rhetorical skills to breathe life into their subjects. These are literary skills that demand imagination. At this point historians are free to exercise their judgement, to decide how they will interpret the evidence, what details they will put in and what they will leave out, and where they will take the story that they are telling.

Practised historians are like master craftsmen seeking to create works that engage readers as they portray the past while seeking to explain and understand it. Their contribution to the intellectual life of a country rests on the applied nature of what they do; a good historian is a concrete not an abstract thinker. A good historian is concerned with the reality in which human beings pass their lives. How then are we to judge and evaluate the contribution that historians make to the intellectual life of a country like Australia?

Let us first consider how the two Greek founders of the art of history understood themselves to be doing. Herodotus explained himself in these terms: 'The purpose is to prevent the traces of human events from being erased by time, and to preserve the fame of the important and remarkable achievements produced by both Greeks and non-Greeks; among the matters covered is, in particular, the causes of the hostilities between Greeks and non-Greeks.'[13] Thucydides says that he began 'the account at the very outbreak of war, in the belief that it was going to be a great war and more worth writing about than any of those that had taken place in the past.'[14]

As human beings we believe that it would be terrible if the accomplishments of our ancestors and our contemporaries were to be obliterated forever, lost in the eddies of time. Before there was history there were epic poems commemorating the great deeds of heroes and gods. History is our means for preventing the loss of the past. Reading Mark Mazower's excellent *Salonica:*

---

13 Herodotus, *The Histories,* Trans. Robin Waterfield, Oxford University Press, Oxford, 1998, p. 3.
14 Thucydides, *History of the Peloponnesian War,* Trans. Rex Warner, Penguin, 1972, p. 35.

City of Ghosts one is struck by how important it was that there be an account of this last refuge of Iberian Jewry, of the home town of Kemal Ataturk, even though the nationalists of modern Greece and Turkey have no interest in its real past.[15]

Still, in a country like Australia, limited in size and resources, we cannot afford to invest in researching, or even teaching, the whole of the human past. It is simply too vast. Like any human community we are left with placing emphasis on what we consider to be our significant past. Our significant past is that section of human history that has particular significance for Australians, it includes both Australian and non-Australian history, and may change as Australia and its place in the world changes.

If we look at the history of 'history' in the Australian context, taking into account both what has been taught and the sorts of things about which Australian historians have written, it can be seen that a number of significant pasts exercised the imagination of these historians. One of these obviously is the history of Australia itself; histories of the various colonies began appearing from a relatively early time. To my mind the most magnificent of these early histories was John West's *History of Tasmania* published in 1852, a liberal history in the best sense of the word, which told the story of Tasmania broadly in terms of the history of liberty but was not afraid to come to terms with the sad story of its Aboriginal population. West was a liberal who appreciated the frailty of the human condition. The best histories have always recognised that there is no pre-ordained plan in history, that there is often an irony

15 Mark Mazower, *Salonica City of Ghosts: Christians, Muslims and Jews 1430–1950*, Harper Perennial, 2005.

in human affairs that defeats any attempt to reduce history to a sermon or to an exercise in moral indoctrination. In the twentieth century it was W.K. Hancock who, in his *Australia* published in 1930, developed the liberal ironic view of Australian history to the highest degree as he outlined how morally earnest Australians pursued justice only to produce something quite different.

British imperial history and Australia's place in empire were, for a long time, at the centre of constituting the significant past in Australia. This was natural given that Britain was the source of much of Australia's culture, laws and political system. In particular there was great interest in the English Revolution of the seventeenth century and its role in the creation of modern democracy. Interestingly there was less interest in the Glorious Revolution of 1688 and the commercial society that it spawned, even though the massive financial and political changes that followed in the wake of 1688 are far more important for understanding Australia than the excesses of Oliver Cromwell. The emphasis on the English Revolution was part of the love affair that many historians in Australia have had with revolution. Unlike America, Australian universities have never taught courses on Western Civilisation and perhaps the study of Britain took over this role in Australia.

European history has also long been taught and studied in Australia with an emphasis on the Renaissance, the Reformation and the modern world since the French Revolution. As well ancient history, in particular the classical world, has long flourished in Australia, in particular in New South Wales. That is not to say that 'big' and world history has not also flourished in Australia. One thinks of Australia's most important internationally twentieth century historian Gordon Childe, or Grafton Eliot Smith. In the 1940s Vere Garnet Portus taught world history at the University of Adelaide. More recently Australia has been home to the most important contemporary practitioner of 'big history', David Christian. Asian history, in particular the history of South East Asia, fostered by government in the national interest, was a latecomer but has flourished over the past fifty years.

What has tended to be missing is interesting. European history tended to downplay the medieval centuries, American history has generated interest but nowhere to the extent that one might have expected; nor has there been enormous interest in either Africa or Latin America. Even the Commonwealth has not struck much of a chord in Australia, Indian history flourished for a while but Canada and South Africa have but rarely excited interest. It is notorious also that Australian and New Zealand historians do not read each others' historiography.

When I began university at the University of Sydney in the 1970s there was coherence to the curriculum. One began with early modern Europe, or medieval Europe, before proceeding to late modern Europe and then completed one's study by looking at either Australia or America. Ancient history lived in its own world, dealing with its own problems, but supported by a relatively strong tradition in Classics. Classes in Latin 1 (composed of students who had passed Latin at the Higher School Certificate) in the early 1970s were attended by more than one hundred students in a lecture theatre.

The last, and perhaps too often overlooked, significant past has been that provided by the Bible, both the old and the new testaments, and more generally the history of the Christian church. Twenty-five years ago history departments in Australian universities had a significant number of priests and former religious working in them including Greg Dening and George Shaw. Moreover many of Australia's leading historians, from Keith Hancock to Manning Clark to Geoffrey Blainey, had clerical fathers. Religious history, including Australian religious history, was a thriving area.

And then there was Australian history. It had a number of interests that included political, economic development, explorers and exploration, the growth of the religious denominations and the emergence and flourishing of the labour movement. Historians of the early twentieth century recognised the centrality of economic factors for any proper appreciation of Australian history, an insight that has been lost in recent times. The two most insightful general histories of Australia, both published in 1930, W.K. Hancock's *Australia* and Edward Shann's *Economic History of Australia* focused on the economic realities of Australian development. They chronicled both the successes and the idiocies in which Australians have indulged from a liberal perspective. In a slightly different way the work of Geoffrey Blainey has continued this tradition of building an interpretation of Australian history by making economic issues central. Blainey has provided many insights into how Australia has been shaped by economic realities, ranging from the 'tyranny of distance' to the importance of the mining industry. But he has been the great outsider of the history profession in Australia. Lesser men and women have seized control of the patronage networks and made the profession in their own images.

Since the highpoint of 1930 in the writing of Australian history it has gone down a number of paths. Particularly significant in this regard were the differences that long existed between the Sydney and Melbourne schools of history. Individual professors were very important until quite late in Australia because there were so few professors. In the 1920s Melbourne-trained historian, and former student of Ernest Scott, Stephen Roberts went to Sydney and in the 1930s Max Crawford, very much in the nonconformist tradition of Sydney historian George Arnold Wood, went to Melbourne. Roberts wrote on Australian land development but also on European history, including *The House that Hitler Built*, a liberal critique of Nazi Germany.

The Sydney tradition combined Australian and European history. In particular European history was, and continues to be, important in New South Wales schools. Roberts' successor J.M. Ward focused on the development of politics in colonial New South Wales but the Department also appointed outstanding scholars from Britain as professors in the field of European (and religious) history, such as John McManners and Patrick Collinson, down to the 1970s. Politically Ward called himself a 'liberal conservative' and the tone of the school was broadly liberal. This liberal culture was reinforced, I believe, by the influence of the philosophy of John Anderson whose realism and classicism stimulated rigorous, and unsentimental, intellectual enquiry. Peter Coleman in 1962 wrote about the counter-revolution in Australian history, alas one that never occurred, based on the work of then young Sydney historians such as Alan Martin and Bruce Mansfield.

The Melbourne school was built by Max Crawford who inherited the strong moralism of Wood, who had opposed the Boer war and written on John Milton. It took the study of history in Melbourne away from the liberal realism that characterised the work of Shann and Hancock and replaced it with a zeal for imposing moral agendas on the world. Crawford could be described as a left liberal and one of his major historical interests was the radicalism and supposed democratic tendencies of the English revolution as exemplified by the Putney debates. The Melbourne school focused much more on British history and Australian history than European history and it combined these concerns with a powerful left wing flavour. It did not look to overseas to leaven its intellectual mix, preferring to employ its own graduates whereas Sydney often told its graduates to look elsewhere for employment. The Melbourne school also sought to colonise the new university departments as they emerged in the 1960s. It had a very strong sense of its own identity and destiny. The result was that the Melbourne school produced a collection of historians who possessed a powerful belief in their moral self-righteousness, were broadly left in their political sympathies, were somewhat narrow in their historical interests and were evangelical in their desire to spread the Melbourne gospel.

The Melbourne school was also broadly in sympathy with Communist historians such as Bob Gollan and Russel Ward who developed the radical nationalist view of Australia that brought together nationalism, radical secularism and the labour movement in a vision of Australian history as social progress that seemed to exclude anyone who was middle class or religious as un-Australian. Russel Ward was the son of a private school Headmaster in Adelaide, just as many Melbourne historians, including Scotch

College alumnus Stuart Macintyre, were products of Melbourne 'public' schools. J.M. Ward in Sydney was proud of his former public high school, Fort Street High.

Manning Clark was both a typical product of the Melbourne history school and yet quite different. It is interesting that although Melbourne historians are willing to defend Clark they have never really approved of his work, not least because he appeared to have retained sympathy for the importance of religion in history. In the same way, that other Melbourne heretic, Geoffrey Blainey, has never really been a member of the club. Clark seemed, in the 1950s and early 1960s, to be something more than just another Melbourne historian, a fresh broom that would sweep the old narrow radical nationalist history away. Peter Coleman wrote in 1962 that Clark 'did more than anyone else to release historians from the prison of radical interpretation.'[16] Clark's proclamation in the first volume of his *History of Australia* that he would study Australian history in terms of its Protestant, Catholic and Enlightenment heritages was bold and appeared to open a new era in the study of Australian history. Likewise the publication of Martin and Loveday's study of factional politics in colonial New South Wales in 1966 promised to inaugurate a new sophistication in the study of Australian political history. At the same time Blainey's work was opening up new ways of seeing Australian history.

But it was a false dawn. What went wrong? It is easy to say 'the sixties' but that would be trite. Rather one should look to the expansion of both secondary education and the universities during

---

16 Peter Coleman, 'Introduction: the new Australia', in Peter Coleman (Ed), *Australian Civilization,* F.W. Cheshire, Melbourne 1963, p. 7.

these years. More students completed high school, more went on to study at university and to become teachers, academics and to staff the ever growing public sector. Previously people practising history in Australia, even at secondary school, had been part of an intellectual elite educated according to exacting standards. First class honours in history, as in other disciplines, were handed out very sparingly.

The democratisation of learning, hand in hand with its rapid expansion, largely destroyed this old elitism (and dramatically increased the number of firsts awarded). There was a rapid expansion of the number of people studying and researching history and of the areas of history that were being studied. This coincided with a world-wide expansion of our knowledge of the past. When he published his classic *The Mediterranean and the Mediterranean world in the Age of Philip II* in 1966, French historian Braudel complained about the lack of knowledge about the Ottoman Empire. Today that is no longer the case. There is now a considerable literature on the Ottomans, as well as on the history of most of the civilised world.

This was also a time when, with Britain entering the Common Market and increasing commercial contacts with Asia, a need was perceived to re-evaluate Australia's intellectual heritage. As well there was a revolt amongst many in the younger generation against what was seen to be the narrow and constricting nature of the Anglo Saxon intellectual tradition. This corresponded with the revival of Marxism with an emphasis on Marxist concepts of culture derived from Gramsci and Lukacs. The consequence was a tendency to adopt ideas enthusiastically and uncritically from the intellectual traditions of continental Europe and to pour scorn on 'empiricism' because of its perceived lack of glamour.

Scholars in areas such as ancient history have always recognised the need to have access to continental scholarship, and they have learnt the languages that provided that access. The new generation of left wing Australian historians invariably read their French and German intellectuals in translation or gained their understanding of them second hand from American textbooks.

The consequence of these developments has been a combination of chaos and anarchy. Some of the results of these changes were as follows:

1. Curricula at universities expanded but lost their rationale and any structure. Offerings became like a smorgasbord from which students picked and chose at their leisure. What was lost was the sense of what a well educated major in history should know. This allowed students to specialise to excess, especially at the larger institutions. At the school level, at least where history has survived as a 'stand alone' subject, curricula have remained more conservative.

2. Australian history has grown in importance. More Australian history is now taught to undergraduates, but most importantly postgraduate research is carried out to a large extent in Australian history. Lacking a language other than English, with British history in decline and surprisingly little interest in American or Commonwealth history, students specialise in Australian history. Hence Australianists have tended to portray the history of history in Australia over the past fifty years as the triumph of Australian history within a more general story of the replacement of dependency on Britain by the emergence of a genuine Australian nationalism.

3. Unfortunately the interest in Australian history has not translated into a greater understanding of Australia's political or economic past. Much Australian political history remains to be written. Economic history has become a lost art. Instead the new generation of Australian historians has largely been pre-occupied with issues raised by the newer fashions in history from North America, in particular social and cultural history, and an obsession with oral history and memory and, of course, there has been a boom in Indigenous history.

4. The consequence is, I believe, that each passing generation of historians produced in Australia has come to know more and more about less and less. The new generation of historians often knows a lot about current trends and fashions in history. They do not generally know much about the past before 1900 or about the traditions of historical writing.

5. Theory has often become more important than practice. By theory I do not mean traditional historiography, the study of historical writing beginning with Thucydides and Herodotus that historians once undertook as a means of improving their craft. Rather I have in mind the obsession with contemporary theory derived in turn from German philosophers with a murky reputation, French gurus attempting to hide their fascist past and the banal ideas of cultural studies. Whereas in 1966 Keith Windschuttle read Gibbon, Macauley, Maitland, Carlyle and Tocqueville as a first year university history student[17] (and students in 1966 were a year younger than today!) contemporary students will be fed a diet of Foucault, radical feminism and Said.

When scholars who have little knowledge of the history of anywhere else but Australia focus their attention on particularly

---

17 Keith Windschuttle, 'Fairer Australis', *Bulletin*, 29 January 2007, http://bulletin.ninemsn.com.au/article.aspx?id=182058

obscure aspects of the social and cultural history of Australia and then use 'theories' of dubious provenance to analyse those aspects what we get are the depressing sets of papers that now dominate the conferences of the Australian Historical Association.

Yet even that is not the whole story. These historians want to make a virtue out of their narrowness. In an article in the *Australian Financial Review*, Richard Bosworth, a renowned historian of fascist Italy at the University of Western Australia, recounted how an Australianist colleague took him to task for being interested in writing for an international audience. Did he not realise, she told him, that he was being funded by the Australian taxpayer? He continues, 'since I have made my career in Australia … I could not be an historian here, unless I was self-consciously nationalised as an Australian'.[18]

Or consider this wonderful piece of know-nothingness by historian Dr Clare Wright:

> There is no question that even after post-graduate training in history, I have emerged with a shaky grasp of the facts. I am a product of a thoroughly post-modern education, schooled to seek and interpret a multiplicity of voices, competing narratives and diverse texts. The order of Australian prime ministers is beyond me; the dates of even key events would see me flailing. But I am also a child of the Information Age. Isn't that why God invented Google?[19]

Of course one must ask: how can someone 'interpret a multiplicity of voices, competing narratives and diverse texts' from a position of ignorance. Surely one can only carry out such a task on the basis

18 Richard Bosworth, 'Killing Histories', *Australian Financial Review*, 25 January 2007.
19 Quoted in Andrew Bolt, 'History in History', *Herald Sun*, 18 August, 2006.

of considerable knowledge of history, including a lot of facts and an experience of human nature. No, what Clare is claiming to be able to use are the tools of a 'post-modern education', a series of questionable and untestable theories, derived from the textbooks of cultural studies. These are abstract and rationalist theories that can be applied as recipes or templates to explain historical events. Historians who rely on such an approach remain trapped within their ideas unable to reach to reach the reality of the past.

A well trained historian capable of writing good history and making a significant contribution to the intellectual life of the country must have more than just a set of abstract theories derived from current fashion. They should have a good knowledge of a range of historical countries and periods, even if they primarily write about Australian history. Instead we are getting the 'Google generation' of historians in Australia, historians who know little outside their particular expertise and yet believe that they have the right to pontificate on all sorts of historical matters. The most extraordinary example of this 'know all' mentality was Stuart Macintyre's inability to get the origins of the word 'history' correct in the *History Wars*.[20]

Again, this is not the whole picture. Anyone who makes a rigorous study of a particular historical issue runs into the problem of moral ambiguity. Historical actors often behave in questionable ways and yet what they end up achieving may possess considerable moral worth. The young Octavian was a rather vicious thug who lied, killed and treated many people in a brutal fashion and yet, as

---

20 Stuart Macintyre and Anna Clark, *The History Wars, 2nd edition,* Melbourne University Press, 2004, p. 16.

Augustus, he brought peace to a Roman world that had suffered almost a century of bloody civil strife. Settlers in Australia could be brutal in their dispossession of the Aboriginal population and yet they brought into being a prosperous country that has helped to feed the world.

It is not the task of the historian to right the wrongs of the past, or to pretend that things could have turned out otherwise, 'if only' someone had behaved differently. Historians are spectators observing events that are often horrible, sometimes despairing, and they can be left marvelling at the excesses of human behaviour or feeling helpless in the wake of the irony of history. This was the great strength of both Hancock and Shann in their writing of Australian history.

We have already noted the moral self-righteousness that characterised the Melbourne school of history. The infection of the historical profession in Australian, in particular Australianists, by the moralistic virus has created an epidemic. There can be no moral ambiguity for these historians; historical events are to be interpreted in black and white moral terms with the values of the early twenty-first century as the measuring rod. History either advances this moral agenda or it impedes it. Hence historical writing becomes both a moral and a political act by which individuals are to be judged, not on the basis of their capacity as historians, but as moral human beings. Matters of intellectual disagreement become the basis of moral condemnation. There is no attempt, for example, to engage with the ideas of Keith Windschuttle, only a desire to condemn him as an immoral human being. There was a precedent for the treatment of Windschuttle in the squalid little volume that appeared in the mid nineteen eighties that attempted to expose how Blainey's historical work was rotten the whole way through.[21]

In the classification of Western culture delineated by John O'Malley many historians in Australia can be seen as falling into the prophecy/reform basket.[22] They see their role as prophets of the nation who must expose the evils of the people so that they can renounce their evil ways and return to righteousness. The first great prophet of Australian history was Manning Clark who increasingly adopted the style and persona of an Old Testament figure. Although historians since Clark have rejected his narrative style of history they have continued to see themselves as being in charge of the conscience of the nation.

As the major sins of the Australian people relate to the past treatment of the Aboriginal people (the White Australia policy runs distant second) this means that Australian historians have been obsessed with Aboriginal history over the past twenty five years. Moreover Aboriginal history fits in well with the postmodern Google historian. For one thing, one does not need to know any history outside of Australian history to practice it. These historians tend to avoid comparative studies and do not ask why, for example, Indian tribes in North America preferred to deal with the British in Canada rather than the Americans.[23] After all, Britain was the devil

---

21 Andrew Markus and M C Ricklefs, (Eds.) *Surrender Australia? Essays in the study and uses of History: Geoffrey Blainey and Asian immigration,* Allen & Unwin, Sydney, 1985.

22 John O'Malley, *Four Cultures of the West,* Harvard University Press, Cambridge Mass, 2004, chapter one.

23 Lawrence H Keeley, *War Before Civilization: The Myth of the Peaceful Savage,* Oxford University Press, New York, 1996, pp. 152–7.

incarnate. Secondly it is fertile ground for the use of post-modern current fashions. Hence historians in this field can argue that oral accounts of events that occurred two hundred years ago are as reliable as written documents or that it doesn't matter if *Terra Nullius* is true or false; what matters is its political significance.

And, of course, that is the problem. Truth, for these historians, is to be evaluated in terms of its political efficacy, not its historical accuracy. The goal is the emancipation of the Australian Aborigines, history is a tool to achieve that goal and it is to be used accordingly. However, when one contemplates the historical fate of the Australian Aborigines, one wonders if history has much to say politically. Like nearly all other hunter gatherers all over the planet, such as the Bushmen, they were the victims of agriculturalists, some of them neither Europeans nor imperialists, eager for land to feed their ever-increasing progeny. Like the Native Americans they were the victims of an enforced isolation that left them exposed to the diseases that ravaged Africa and Eurasia. There is much in our explorations of the past that we find to be cruel, brutal and unfair. It is arrogant hubris for anyone to believe that he or she has the power to undo this unfairness.

Now all of this would not matter much if history in Australia was simply a hobby like stamp-collecting or steam trains. But history is considered to be much more than this, both by ordinary Australians and their governments. Keith Hancock once wrote that Australians do not much like economists. The same is not true of historians. There are prizes for historical writing offered by nearly every state government and by the Commonwealth government. Premiers and prime ministers have been known to take a personal interest in fostering the writing and teaching of history, especially Australian history. Historians from Manning Clark to Geoffrey Blainey to Henry Reynolds and Keith Windschuttle are discussed in the media to a degree that the members of no other intellectual discipline enjoy.

However, in one way, these high profile historians differ from their counterparts in Britain. They have not become television stars, unlike Niall Ferguson or David Starkey or Simon Schama. Since *The Blainey View*, derided by his academic colleagues at the University of Melbourne, no major documentary series based around a particular historian has been attempted. Historical celebrities achieve their status in Australia through writing in newspapers, appearing on discussion programs on radio and television, and giving lectures at arts festivals. Often it is not so much the substance of what they have to say that appears before the public as their conflicts and disputes.

Some historians have achieved public influence in another way. When the Commonwealth government began to take an active interest in civics education in the early 1990s it looked to historians rather than political scientists, or even historians with a competence in political science, to compose its advisory and expert committees. This was odd given the decline in political history as a field of inquiry amongst members of the historical profession. In fact, the situation had been reached in which it was a political journalist, Paul Kelly, who wrote what has become the standard political history of Australia in the 1980s.

What this meant is that a small number of historians, had an enormous influence on the whole development of the civics education program run by the Commonwealth Department of Education, especially the *Discovering Democracy* program of the late 1990s. Given the lack of expertise amongst these historians in political science and political theory it is not to be wondered that there were significant deficiencies in the program. The program was characterised by a rather simplistic majoritarian view of democracy combined with a Whig history approach to the development of democracy in Australia. Key aspects of liberal democracy such as the operation of the rule of law and the protection of individual liberties and private property had little or no place in the program. Democracy tended to be measured in such terms as the extension of the franchise. The idea of democracy was not explored with any great sophistication.

There were, in fact, many problems with *Discovering Democracy*. These may be attributed to the hold that the Department and its advising historians had over the process. One was the way in which non-republicans, despite the results of the 1999 referendum, were shut out of making significant contributions to the program, as were the many religious groups who correctly wanted the contribution of Christianity to the development of the Australian political system given its due. Even the flag was given a rough ride until the Flag Association managed to get hold of then Minister of Education, Brendan Nelson.

One can see similarities to *Discovering Democracy* in the curriculum developed by the New South Wales government under Bob Carr for the compulsory study of history and civics in schools for years nine and ten. The curriculum again had a somewhat simplistic model of political development that had an almost exclusively secular focus and concentrated on topics such as the Vietnam War and the Whitlam Government. Once Whitlam had departed the scene it was at a loss to know what to do with the Australian story so it ignored the economic reforms of the 1980s and concentrated on social movements such as feminism.

Although historians in Australia may not be media stars like their British counterparts, they nevertheless possess a public profile and a political influence that exceeds what one might expect. There have been 'history wars' in Australia but not 'English wars' or 'political science wars'. This is because of the special place that history appears to have in Australian public and intellectual life; great things are expected of historians in Australia and the historians also believe that they have a special role, a prophetic role. Working as both an historian and a political scientist I'm often intrigued by the fact that historians have a sense of their own importance, their moral superiority and sense of mission that political scientists seem to lack.

Of course when one has an excessive pride in what one does the consequence is very often hubris. The role that Australian historians have played in the development of civics and history education over the past fifteen years indicates to me that that hubris has not necessarily resulted in benefits for the public. It would have been far better if there had been fewer historians involved in civics education and if the mix of people involved had included not only political scientists but also other educated Australians. Historians in Australia who specialise in Australian history often have a very narrow understanding of history that does not extend much beyond the boundaries of Australia. Their knowledge and understanding of Western intellectual traditions is also generally not vast. Moreover this narrow knowledge is generally matched by a narrowness of outlook, as Professor Bosworth discovered when he engaged a senior Australianist in conversation, and an evangelical zeal to have their viewpoint become the dominant one.

The truth is that historians have assumed a prophetic role in Australian culture, and have been recognised as prophets by both commentators and the general public. For someone like myself, who much prefers Erasmus to Savonarola, and finds irony rather than denunciation an appropriate means of dealing with human history, the idea of the historian as prophet is not very attractive. Knowing that many of these prophet historians have little knowledge of anything outside Australia and are often imprisoned inside their abstract theories makes it even less attractive. One can only think that there must be a better way.

The best historians are not really intellectuals in the more pejorative sense of the word. They are not, and should not, be addicted to abstract ideas and Jacobin schemes in politics. A historian should be highly skilled in the intellectual and affective capacities required to explore, explain and understand the past. To achieve this level of skill the historian should study a number of periods and places, read as widely as possible in great historical literature, and have at least have some facility with a language other than English. The bar is high but then the vocation of being an historian should be considered as one that requires considerable effort on the part of one who seeks to join the ranks of the profession.

Now there are still parts of the historical profession that lives up to this ideal. But, alas, this cannot be said of those who take the easy path to specialise in Australian history. Too many of these have become postmodern Google historians who parade their ignorance and attempt to compensate for it by a mixture of faddish ideas, moral self-righteousness and political activism. The result is an Australian history that is intellectually impoverished, preferring to substitute political correctness for the rigorous skills of scholarship. This is happening at a time when, with the massive changes that have taken place over the past forty years, Australians need to consider what constitutes their 'significant past', both in terms of what is taught and what is researched. Australian historians would have Australian students simply study Australia, an Australia defined by their political and ideological preoccupations.

The poverty of their ambitions can be seen in the outcome of the Australian History Summit held in August 2006. The majority of the Summit, faced by a proposal that sought to embed the study of Australian history in its wider context and to revivify the practice of narrative history, preferred to accept the argument of those who were ideologically opposed to such an idea that it was too demanding to teach. In its place they adopted the 'questions' approach to the study of Australian history, a dumbed down, simplistic picture of Australian history. This failure can largely be attributed to the failure of the then Minister to appreciate the politics of the history profession and the difficulty involved in managing the process. Instead, by putting forward the idea that the Summit represented the 'sensible centre', legitimacy was given to those participants attending the Summit who were neither of the centre nor sensible.

The history of what occurred subsequent to the Summit indicates how deep the problems of the study and teaching of Australian history have become. In order to retrieve the situation the then Prime Minister John Howard created a small committee to review what the Summit and the sub-committee that succeeded it had produced. The Prime Minister's committee was attacked for supposed bias. What it produced, however, was less remarkable for its confusion than for any bias. It tried to make some sense out of the need to reconcile narrative history with the vague themes and issues recommended by the Summit. The result was a mish mash that was quite unsatisfying, not least because it put forward the idea that Australian history be studied with only minimum reference to the rest of the world. At that point the Coalition Government lost power in 2007.

The Labor Government still wanted history to be a core element of the school curriculum. It subsequently moved away from teaching just Australian history and proposed in its place a mixture of global history and Australian history. The move away from an exclusive focus on Australian history was a positive move as the history of one's country can only be understood when it is placed in a broader context. The idea seemed to be a good one, even if responsibility for the curriculum was placed in the hands of Professor Stuart Macintyre. However, the process of curriculum development soon spiraled out of control.

What occurred was a seemingly endless round of consultations with a whole range of people, the so-called stakeholders, regarding the content of the curriculum. It developed as a bureaucratic exercise conducted by the Australian Curriculum, Assessment and

Reporting Authority or ACARA. I have had some involvement in this process. I attended three sessions in 2010 at which groups composed of people from all around Australia came together and provided comments on selected aspects of the curriculum. The groups were composed of educational bureaucrats and school teachers, and I must admit that I came to appreciate the enthusiasm and professionalism of those teachers. Outside of history educators there has not been very much involvement by academic historians. The scope of these sessions was limited to technical rather than intellectual issues.

When the draft curriculum was released for comment in 2010 it was attacked by a variety of people, including the Federal Opposition. The Opposition Education spokesman, Christopher Pyne, argued that it over emphasised Indigenous culture while ignoring Magna Carta. He also criticised the emphasis on Asia at the expense of Australia's Western heritage. Conservative education commentator Kevin Donnelly made similar criticisms. Like Pyne he was concerned about the emphasis on Asia and Indigenous perspectives instead of the European traditions that have moulded Australia's institutions. Mervyn Bendle criticised the curriculum as constituting an attack on the Australian military history and in particular on the ANZAC tradition.

Nevertheless it would be true to say that the release of the National Curriculum did not ignite a new significant round of the History Wars. Given the bare bones of the curriculum document it was difficult to discern a lot that could be could be described as outlandishly ideological. One could see ideological touches here and there, such as in the implication that the settlement of

Australia was an imperial response to the Industrial Revolution and its view that human rights wee a creation of the United Nations, but it was difficult to pin them down. A complicating factor was that a range of people have been involved in writing the different parts of the curriculum such that it lacked an overall coherence and consistency. There were problems with the document but they were not ones that were amenable to a History Wars style response.

The problems were structural in nature and related to the attempt to have a world history approach while at the same time emphasising the national history of Australia. These can be seen in two very practical matters:

- How does one decide what to put in and what to leave out?
- How does one balance the need to create some sort of narrative with the need to look at some issues in depth?

These are important issues as the time that can be devoted to history in a 'crowded' curriculum is limited. At every stage of the process from the 2006 Summit onwards teachers have complained that the amount of material proposed to be taught is too great. They have also indicated that they prefer to teach about some matters in depth. It is interesting that some of the major complaints about the new curriculum came from the History Teacher's Association, on the ground that the curriculum covers too much material, and from some of the State Education Departments.

The real problem for any history curriculum, especially in an age in which historical knowledge has exploded, is to have clear principles regarding the selection of material. If there is only a limited amount that the curriculum can cover how are we to decide what those topics should be? Unfortunately there was no discussion of what principles should be applied to achieve this aim. Instead the curriculum grew like topsy in response to particular criticisms and specific concerns of some individuals and groups. As mentioned previously one constraining element was the need to comply with the Indigenous, Asian and sustainability foci.

As an interested observer the development of the curriculum looked to me like an example of that organised chaos of which only bureaucracies are capable. One major issue relates to the need to have both a general narrative, described as an overview, and a series of areas of more intensive study, or what are called depth studies. The overviews became essentially a list of events, and one might well ask if these lists provide students with a coherent map of the past. The depth studies are in many ways a strange collection of topics and it is conceivable that a student could come out of studying history at high school with knowledge about a disconnected, even bizarre, set of places and historical periods. The depth studies include Polynesian expansion across the Pacific, the Khmer Empire, the Mongols, the Black Death and a comparison of a nineteenth century Australian city with an Asian city.

Australian history is covered in two ways. It forms the basis of the primary school history curriculum. At high school it is only really covered in the final two years of compulsory schooling, still in tandem with world history. There is a substantial concentration in the Australian history depth studies on World War I and Australia's involvement in other twentieth century wars. The battle for Indigenous rights, although placed alongside other civil rights movements, constitutes another depth study. The feminist movement, along with Australian popular culture (Kylie and AC/

DC studies?), are also there along with a study of the environmental movement. What is missing is much consideration of Australian political history, and there is hardly anything on the economic development of the country.

My major criticism of the National History Curriculum is not that it is excessively ideological, although there are issues in that area, but that it is a dog's breakfast. And this again raises the important issue about what the sort of history being taught to students in a country like Australia, should look like.

We inhabit national entities that are part of a global community. It is highly laudable that our students should have an understanding of the way in which human history has developed over the past few thousand years. We need to understand and appreciate our national history. How do we do it?

In one sense this also goes back to the role that history is meant to play in the curriculum as a compulsory area of study. Why is it there? This issue has not really been addressed in Australia. Of course, good reasons can be given; and I think that they have to do with providing students with the opportunity to explore human beings and human behaviour and to think deeply about what it means to be human.

As mentioned earlier. I have made a modest attempt to suggest a principle that could be used as a guide to deciding what should go into such a curriculum. It is what I term the 'significant past' which is to say the past that is important for a particular country or nation. The point is that we cannot teach everything. We can only teach that which is significant and which has relevance for students. Such an approach goes back to the dawn of historical writing as Herodotus conducted his inquiries into those matters that helped to explain the Persian Wars.

To me this means providing students with an appreciation of the broad set of factors that have shaped human history, from climate to economics to warfare to ideas and beliefs to the role of individuals. It would mean focusing on those parts of history that enable students to understand how the nation of which they are part came to be the way that it is. In the case of Australia this means that there would be little taught, for example, about either Africa or South America. Europe and East Asia would loom large and North America would have a place. Of course Australian Indigenous history would have its proper and rightful place.

But, unlike the current curriculum, there would need to be an emphasis placed on Australia's European, and specifically British, heritage. It is simply foolish to mandate Indigenous history and the study of Asia and to leave out the European dimension of Australian history. They all have to be there. Anecdotal evidence suggests that students in the past have not taken kindly to an excessive emphasis on Indigenous history, especially when the same material has been taught at a number of levels. One thing that the new curriculum does is to eliminate this sort of repetition.

Students have also tended to find Australian history 'boring' in comparison to the history of other places. After all, the history of non-Indigenous Australia has largely been the story of economic development and the peaceful growth of democratic institutions. It has sometimes been the complaint that the problem with Australian history is that it does not have a revolution. This probably explains why students are generally attracted to the study of Australia's role in the wars of the twentieth century and why this aspect of Australian history is given such prominence in the curriculum.

Ultimately how the curriculum will be taught will depend on the teachers themselves and not, as some suggest, on those who have been nominally in charge of the process. The curriculum sets out the bare bones of what is to be taught. It is up to the teachers to put the flesh on it. There will be those who will use it as an opportunity for putting a partisan case to the students but there are also many teachers with high professional standards. The real problem will come when teachers with inadequate historical training are put in front of a class that needs to be convinced that the study of history is worth the effort.

The History Wars helped to create the environment in which history achieved its new and somewhat unexpected status as one of the four pillars of the new National Australian Curriculum. But this has meant that there has been little constructive discussion regarding the principles that should underpin this curriculum. The consequence is, I believe, a muddle. A 'History Wars' style of approach such as that of Mervyn Bendle who at one stage 'declared war on ACARA' is not very helpful. My feeling is that we will get an unsatisfactory curriculum but, Australia being Australia, the focus will be on practical matters such as how to provide adequate training for those teachers who will have to teach this curriculum.

If one does not have clear and well enunciated set of ideas about what one is doing then it will be the 'process' that will determine how the curriculum will turn out. This is the process of reshaping through consultation with stakeholders, and of development by bureaucrats. Such a process takes on a life of its own that, I fear, takes it almost beyond human hands.

One of the real problems with the way in which history is written and taught in Australia is the way in which historians have assumed the prophet's mantle. This enables them to do two things. The first is to reduce the historical story to a simple Manichean tale in which it is possible to identify the evil ones. The overwhelming desire to engage in moral denunciation and the tendency to simplify go together. Once an element of complexity has been established it is no longer possible see the past in simple moralistic terms and then to engage in moral self-righteousness. The fact is that human beings are complex entities who have both created things of great beauty and done terrible deeds. The Parthenon of Athens was made possible by the revenue generated by Athenian imperialism. That fact does not make it any less an extraordinary achievement. The role of the historian is to understand the people of the past, to analyze why they behaved in the way that they did and to enter into an imaginative empathy with them.

Students love to study history. They are attracted by the great individuals, the stories of extraordinary achievement and tragedy. They also know when they are being fed politicised garbage disguised as history. There is no agenda in ancient history, just a world in which they are free to explore human beings and their lives. That is why the study of the ancient world is so popular in New South Wales. There should be no agenda in the study of modern and Australian history. Otherwise the historical profession will have failed in its calling.

The study of Australian history at Australian universities is clearly in trouble.[24] Enrolments are down and it appears that the students of twenty-first century Australia are more interested in studying global history than the history of their own country. That students have an interest in the history of the wider world is a positive thing; that they should be shunning the study of their own country is not. They should be interested in both. It is not a matter of students becoming more internationally focused and renouncing the nationalism of former generations. Looking at how the younger generation now celebrates Australia Day one can only conclude that they are more, not less, nationalistic than their predecessors. So what is going on?

Comments made by Professor Marilyn Lake quoted in the *Australian* provide a clue: 'Student whims are determining what is taught and therefore who is employed. This isn't a very rational and scholarly way to approach university education.'[25] Apparently Professor Lake believes that students have no right to choose what they would like to study. It must be left up to people like Professor Lake to choose for them. Professor Lake's view was supported by Professor Stuart Macintyre who, in a subsequent article, argued that 'disciplines judged to be important cannot be left to the vagaries of the market.'[26] Professor Lake doesn't seem to get it. Students have listened to Professor Lake, her friends and acolytes in the universities and schools and decided that they do not like what they hear. And why should they? Who wants to sit in a class and hear their country

---

24 Much of the following passage appeared in Greg Melleuish, 'Time to take the black armband off,' *Spectator*, 21 April 2012.

25 Andrew Trounson, ' Students feel the weight of history,' *Australian*, 29 February 2012.

26 Andrew Trounson, 'Why our history's losing its lustre,' *Australian*, 7 March, 2012.

being constantly rubbished and denigrated? Who wants to hear stories about how evil their ancestors were and what terrible crimes they committed?

Despite Professor Macintyre's comments it is not the duty of the government to support 'important' disciplines if they are badly taught and alienate students so that they run away in droves. This is typical of the academic mentality. Everyone is to blame for our problem but us. It's a bit like the old way protection worked in Australia. An industry was performing badly so the solution was to slap a tariff on imports in that industry. The consequence was even poorer performance. If Australian history is performing badly then Australian historians need to shoulder the blame. They cannot go to the Minister with special pleading. They have to change their ways. Professor Lake's comments seem to imply that the 'rational and scholarly way' is to restrict student choice so that they cannot avoid imbibing a mixture of a denunciation of the crimes of the past and a 'progressive ideology' that will show the way to a far better future. The only problem is that students do not want to be indoctrinated. They want to study history and they want it not only to be interesting but taught by people who have a love for the subject. Consider the case of ancient history in New South Wales which we have already discussed. Students coming to university want to study ancient history. This is not a 'whim.' They have been taught at school by teachers who love the ancient world and who have instilled a similar love in them. Ancient history is extremely popular both as a Higher School Certificate subject and as a university subject in New South Wales. It has been claimed that one of the reasons why universities are backward in offering Australian history in first year is that students have studied it at school and are tired of it. Why then are students who studied ancient history at school similarly not tired of it? They have had a taste of it, liked it and want more. It is simply the case that ancient history appeals while Australian history has a sour taste. Of course the problem is not Australian history but the way in which it is taught. What students are tired of is being told how awful their forebears were, which by implication also means them. Young people are not moving away from the study of Australian history because they are less nationalistic than previous generations but because they have a pride in their nation. It has been reported that Australian history is thriving at the University of New England. We need to know why that is the case but one can only suspect that it is taught in an appealing way. Another part of Professor Lake's statement gives a real indication of her real concerns. 'Whim' will have an impact on 'who is employed.' Academia is ultimately about power and patronage. If there are no students studying Australian history then there are no jobs for those who have done PhDs in the area. That means no jobs for those who have chosen to study under the 'stars' of Australian history. Across the country there is a veritable army of postgraduate students writing theses on Australian topics. There are far fewer doing non-Australian topics. Under current conditions there will be no academic positions for these students who have devoted three years of their lives to becoming experts in some small corner of the history of Australia. A real problem is that, unlike America where postgraduates must study areas outside of their research area so they can teach in these areas, in Australia postgraduates generally know only about the country they are studying. They are very narrowly trained. Their knowledge of global history and the history of other parts of the world is slight. They tend not to have studied a language other than English.

The problem that has emerged in recent years has been less one of ideology than trivialisation. The coming generation of Australian historians is not interested in big questions of history, even in the Australian context, but with relatively obscure aspects of social and cultural history. I recently came across a research project on wedding cakes in Australia. They also have problems dealing with the most recent period of Australian history which has become the preserve of journalists such as Paul Kelly and George Megalogenis. I looked through recent programs of the Australian Historical Association conferences and found that a lot of the papers focused on the period 1870 to 1940. In this period aspiring historians can apply the tired out old categories of race, class and gender to topics of increasing insignificance. This also means that cotemporary Australian history is largely ignored, partly because it does not fit into their ideological straightjacket. But it is the period that is most relevant for the young people of today. It makes more sense to recruit historians to teach those areas that students want to study from outside of Australia. The 'whims' of students threaten the academic empires which Australian historians have built up over the past twenty-five years. In simple terms Australian historians have been mugged by reality. In the heady days, some twenty years ago, they thought that they would conquer the Australian universities, to be followed by the schools. Their 'black armband' version of Australian history would become 'hegemonic' and their troops of disciples would continue down the path that they had forged. Now it is all coming apart. As the Lakes, Macintyres and Reynolds shuffle off the stage towards the inevitable 'Sans teeth, sans eyes, sans taste, sans everything' it appears that their legacy will not be as they intended. And it all comes down to student choice. No one wants to study something that is being trashed. If they are given the chance they will choose to study something which is loved by those who have been entrusted with its care. In the short term Professor Lake is correct. There will be a lot of unhappy young people who have undertaken the study of Australian history in the hope of an academic career. Given conditions in other countries there will be more academic positions in history going to applicants from overseas. There will be fewer opportunities for patronage. Hopefully academic historians in Australia will take a long hard look at themselves. They must recognise that students need to study global history, the history of Western civilisation as well as Australian history. They must change the way in which academic historians are trained. And they must come to understand that it is love of a subject that inspires students. Black armband history leads only to ruin.

I may have painted the situation in Australian history as far more dire than is the case but there is no doubt that the study of Australian history is in real crisis. And the source of that crisis must be sheeted back to those who have run their academic empires over the past forty years.

The study of history provides a striking example of how intellectual life has developed in Australia in recent times. There is a 'history subculture' sustained by academia and its ancillaries. It has adopted a set of ideas to which any individual must subscribe if they are to achieve preferment within the academic world. Despite its declining financial benefits there are still many more people in search of employment in history departments than there are positions. This is especially the case in Australian history. Buck the party line and you won't even get a first foot on the ladder. Under such circumstances any talented person would seek more lucrative employment elsewhere.

This victory of mind over matter is hardly healthy for any sort of intellectual life in Australia. It means that there is a set of attitudes, a cast of mind outside which one must not stray if one wants to be considered part of the club. If you don't conform you are not simply someone who holds a different interpretation; you are not worthy of the name historian. This was the tactic that was employed consistently against Keith Windschuttle, even though he was far better credentialed than others who were called historians.

Of course, it could be argued that history is the most extreme case of intellectual bigotry and conformity in Australia. Certainly, from my experience, it is much more intolerant than political science. In general, I believe, the humanities are much worse than the social sciences in terms of narrowness of attitude and intolerance of intellectual difference. The reason for this is that the humanities have gone further down the track of not being concerned about empirical evidence and foregoing analytical rigour when using argument. They have fallen into the trap of believing that all they need is good rhetoric which, of course, is just a more fancy word for spin.

The real problem is how to remedy this situation and to restore a genuine pluralism in Australian intellectual life. I do not believe that there is much hope in reforming the existing institutions. Academics, who are the most conservative of people when it comes to defending their patch, will fight a savage rearguard action. Rather strategies must be developed for the creation of alternatives to the status quo. This means creating books and documentaries that provide a view of both history and the humanities more generally that is not dictated by the subculture group think. It means creating institutions that will employ people who are seen as beyond the pale by the intellectual establishment.

The task is not an easy one. But the alternative is much, much worse. Despite all the rhetoric about the Howard years having turned things around, my belief is that the last ten years has only seen a continuation of trends that had already been in train for twenty years. There is a logic in a small country like Australia that tends to lead to the creation of cartels that dominate intellectual life. The challenge is to create a 'level playing field' in which there is a genuine competition of ideas. This is one of the conditions of a healthy democratic society.

Epilogue:
An Alternate Vision

It is one thing to criticise the way in which things have developed in the past. It is quite another to formulate a positive vision for the intellectual life of the future. We know where things have gone wrong. We could spend our time denouncing that situation and feeling good about how we have avoided pitfalls. That way lies the comfort of the 'holy huddle', of the 'saving remnant' that believes that it can be saved just by being a remnant.

The real task ahead is to provide an alternative program that can be taken up by those who wish to escape the clutches of the tyranny of Left hegemony.

It may correctly be said that the person who owns the past invariably owns the future. Australian intellectuals have correctly recognised that history is the key discipline for both understanding culture and pointing the direction in which culture should move. For there is a very important fact in these matters which is that it is impossible for every aspect of human knowledge to be readily available in the public sphere and to be taught and researched in educational institutions. There is almost too much knowledge about human beings and their societies and cultures and that knowledge has exploded over the past fifty years.

Traditionally the high culture of a civilisation was marked by a thorough knowledge of a limited number of texts. There was time when intellectual training consisted in both analyzing texts and being able to write a commentary on them. This may sound dry but it encouraged students to develop intensively their intellectual capacities in a way that is no longer possible. The British Empire was run by men who had a very good knowledge of a number of Greek and Latin texts. One central element of their education lay in their capacity to perfect the art of prose composition. This required them to take a piece of English, usually something like a speech of Fox or Burke, and to render it into Greek or Latin in the style of a particular author, be it Cicero or Thucydides. Today such an exercise would be described as lacking utility, but it was an activity that required considerable intellectual accomplishment and those trained in this way gained much mental agility. It also allowed them to enlarge their concentration, to be precise and to present arguments in a logical and clear fashion.

Of course, in the modern world, it is no longer possible to train a single, unified elite in such a fashion. Our world is too complex; it requires a number of elites, each with its own specialised body of knowledge. Even within the humanities, the amount of specialisation is so great that it is difficult to discern a body of knowledge or texts that would be shared by all who saw themselves as engaged in studying the humanities. Nevertheless the issue of a shared cultural literacy, a set of shared knowledge, remains important. Some time ago I mentioned Goethe to a class of Politics students, only to discover that no-one in the class had heard of him. I now understand that most of my students do not have anything that resembles a workable map of the past or a general appreciation of the bare bones of Western civilisation. I had a student who asked if the Glorious Revolution of 1688 took place during the Wars of the Roses.

Cultivating an understanding of history and the issue of a common set of texts that form the basis of an awareness of culture are entwined with each other. For there to be some sort of moral and cultural conversation in which everyone can participate there needs to be both a shared appreciation of the past and a common set of texts that can provide models and examples. There was a time when much of this common cultural inheritance was provided by the Bible, the Greek and Latin classics, classical history and some English history and literature. This is why the English language is studded with quotes from Shakespeare, the Bible and other English and classical sources. Today many people use the same quotes without being aware of their source. In nineteenth century Australia Charles Badham commented that perhaps the classics were too difficult for colonials and that they should concentrate on English literature, in particular Shakespeare and Milton.

Of that complex cultural inheritance only Shakespeare really survives as a real cultural presence. School students generally encounter some portion of Shakespeare in their study. They will not read much else in the way of the classics of English literature, they will not know much about the classical world, the Bible or English or European history. There are those who say that this is a good thing as they can instead refer to episodes in *The Simpsons* or some other part of popular culture. The problem is that popular culture is transitory; what is known to one generation is forgotten by the next as I recently discovered when I mentioned Laurel and Hardy to a class. The advantage of a classic of literature is that it has stood the test of time and can be transmitted from one generation to the next. Of course, such transmission does not work if those who are responsible for this most important of roles neglect their responsibility and pursue instead the fleeting and the trivial as today often seems to be the case.

Much has been lost. It can be claimed that we are now living in the senescence of a culture that has lost its power to move us or to provide much in the way of a model for our actions. The age appears to be approaching when young people will sit in the ruins of Western civilisation unable to understand or to appreciate the messages that are to be found in its great works of art and literature. Instead they will simply rejoice in the banality of whatever the current popular form of culture provides for them. Essentially they will be people without a past, living in a perpetual present, trapped in that present and unable to enter into the most important conversations that human beings have held about themselves, the world and ultimate reality.

We can either acquiesce in this situation, recognising that it is part of the ultimate fate of any civilisation, or we can attempt to repair some of the structures. It is clear that we cannot go back to some ideal model that existed as recently as the early twentieth century. That has gone. It is also clear that we need to re-consider what we must continue to preserve at all costs and to what we must bid farewell. Ernst Curtius once wrote that to appreciate the classical European tradition one needed to know both Latin and all the Romance languages. Such an ideal today is not possible. We need a robust model for the twenty-first century. But we must repair the ramparts.

What this means above all is deciding what we can and should maintain, and providing the means whereby it can be transmitted to future generations. The idea of a canon has always involved deciding what works really matter and are therefore worthy of study. We need such a canon for the twenty-first century. Of course there will be disagreements about who should be in and who should be out but there will be a core that most people will recognise is essential. In an English speaking society it will always include Shakespeare and it should include Milton. It will also include Homer, Plato, Aristotle, Virgil and Cicero, Dante and Goethe, figures of great stature because they tell us so much about the human condition.

The other important matter is finding the means whereby young people can gain access to these great works. In many places schools and universities are pre-occupied with the trivia of popular culture. Philosophers are concerned with the fashionable issues of the moment and neglect the history of philosophy. Historians no longer require students to read the classic works of history. The study of languages focuses on being able to speak the language and no longer has literature as its central focus. Australian academics and intellectuals continue to fail to live up to their task of preserving and transmitting the best that has been thought and written.

There are rare beacons of light. Some are found hidden in the dark corners of our sandstone universities. A major one can be found in Campion College which has devised a curriculum that will introduce undergraduate students to the history and traditions of Western Civilisation. There is some ground for hope. But if we are to undo the century of harm that has been inflicted by many Australian intellectuals on culture in Australia we need to take positive steps to counter that harm and to provide our young people with the opportunity to explore the great works of the civilisation of which Australia is still a part.